INSIDE GRIEF

INSIDE GRIEF

DEATH, LOSS AND BEREAVEMENT
AN ANTHOLOGY

WITH FOREWORDS BY

STANLEY A. TERMAN, Ph.D., M.D.
AND
VENERABLE DR. METTANANDO BHIKKHU

EDITED

BY

LINE WISE

Wise Press — Incline Village, Nevada

Wise Press, Incline Village, Nevada 89450
First Edition
Printed in the United States of America

ISBN 0-9705708-0-5

Library of Congress Catalog Number: 00-109792

06 05 04 03 02 2001   5 4 3 2 1

Cover by G. Lloyd Solly II

To order additional copies of INSIDE GRIEF or for information
regarding future projects please visit our website:
www.wisepress.com or write to us at:
Wise Press
P. O. Box 180928
Coronado, CA 92178

For David

In Memory of
Eugenia M. Wise
1920 – 2000

About the Editor

LINE WISE is pursuing her Masters Degree at the University of Southern California Andrus School of Gerontology. She combines her background as a poet with the study of gerontology to bring awareness and understanding to issues related to aging.

Contents

FOREWORDS

"Heart-to-heart," —a most overused expression

Yet, how else can I express the mechanism of impact of Line Wise's *Inside Grief*?

I cannot imagine a non-fiction "how to" book dealing with the subject of death and mourning as impactfully. Although the experience is universal, it affects each of us differently. Consider this example from Robert Waters Grey's *Triple Digits*, about a mother who suffers from Alzheimer's Disease:

> doctors rewarded your flesh,
> which clung like a hidebound
> curse, for its backbone, by
> offering coumadin to prevent
> another stroke, even though
> your brain seldom urged your
> limbs to stir or told your
> tongue to fashion sounds
> which mimicked words.

I found it easy to share why I could relate to this passage; I'm a doctor who abhors futile treatment. But other passages affected me even more deeply and more personally, because they gave me glimpses of what my own experience of death and grieving will some day be like.

Line Wise's approach is both simple and brilliant. If the experience is universal, why not ask the articulate among us to share theirs? Others will play music, build skyscrapers, even prescribe coumadin. But if we are searching for emotional impact, we must read the words of those who can write. Ms. Wise screened no less than twenty thousand writing samples from all over the English-speaking world to select the forty-four works which now appear in her anthology. I doubt if there are any among us who will not be moved by many of their stories and poems.

Stanley A. Terman, Ph.D., M.D.

"Who am I? Why am I here in this world? What is life all about?"

Often, we wait to face such profound questions until we are in the midst of grief or crisis. For some, answers are readily found in the beliefs of their religion or philosophy. For others, solace is found by sharing with closest friends. But for many, when pain lasts long and causes agitation and despair, still more is needed. The sharing of universal experiences and the implicit advice found in *Inside Grief* can fill that need.

Since pain is inescapable, we should strive to become stronger because of it. One of the earliest stories of transcending pain is the tale of Kisa Gotami, a young mother who had just lost her baby. Stricken with grief, she could not cope with the fact that her baby was dead. She refused to listen to anyone who advised her to face her loss. She traveled to the Buddha from afar, hoping his wisdom and power would somehow create a miracle. Making her way through the crowd of listeners that surrounded the Buddha, she finally came to face him. Holding the dead baby in her arms, she pleaded with him to revive it from death. The Buddha did not refuse her; instead, he asked her to perform a ritual and bring him a remedy. She was to visit the homes in the village, ask them if they had any mustard seeds, and then bring him one mustard seed from the first home in which no one had died for three generations.

The bereaving mother spent the whole day walking from home to home. Almost every family on whose door she knocked had mustard seeds, but when they were asked whether there was someone who died there in the past three generations, they all shook their heads sadly. There was no home in which death had not visited. Exhausted and full of despair, she returned to the Buddha for his advice. She began to realize that death is part of life and came to appreciate the Buddha's wisdom for prescribing this ritual. Ultimately, she became one of the most outstanding of the Buddha's enlightened disciples.

Pain has the potential to sharpen our mind with wisdom. Sharing love and sympathy based on individual experiences is the finest path to renew the spirit and to regain happiness.

As I read Line Wise's *Inside Grief,* I was touched in various ways: the diversity of experiences, the intense emotions, and the lessons of coping—all reached me in diverse but articulate styles. No ordinary book, this is a collection of life experiences that every member of the human race must face, like Kisa Gotami.

When I finished Wise's book, there was no miracle, nor did I finally have the definitive answers to the fundamental questions of life. But I did feel enriched by the impact of these shared stories and poems, which made me feel stronger and spiritually nourished.

I offer thanks to Line Wise for her industry in collecting and editing this marvelous collection.

Venerable Dr. Mettanando Bhikkhu

PREFACE

The stories and poems in this anthology reflect universal experiences articulated by some of the most talented poets and writers in the English-speaking world. How were forty-four selected from the twenty thousand submissions? By a single criterion: emotional impact. The result is a variety of extremely candid, heartfelt and deeply touching portraits that speak to pertinent issues about which we fear most: loss of our minds (dementia), loss of our loved ones, and loss of control (being subject to the whims of doctors in hospitals). But the emotions not only include anger, rage, confusion, depression and fear; hope, love and spiritual growth can also accompany the challenges surrounding end-of-life experiences.

By encouraging us to embrace a language of sympathy, these stories and poems can help us all gain insight, develop deeper understanding, open new channels of communication and evolve spiritually. The readings thus widen our own direct experiences and prepare us for the ultimate one which we must all someday face.

I thank the many writers who have shared their stories and poetry. Your writings have touched me deeply.

My deepest gratitude goes to those who have helped bring this anthology together: Don Eddy for his assistance with editing, review and the countless details, and Lloyd Solly who brought his creativity, insight and understanding into the design of the cover.

And to my family, whose love supports me.

THE WONDERING

CAROLYN BRIGIT FLYNN

HOSPITAL GUARD

Is this how it was for you?
Watching over us through kindergarten's fence,
rushing to protect from bullies
and rough-handed adults?
I sit night watch, guarding
against nurses with pinpricks
and beeping machines,
who may or may not
have hands of grace. I've learned
to present my daughter-bear intentions early,
call out orders before they near your bed.
And yet it is impossible,
as you must have learned all those years ago,
to keep you from your life.

Here on my trembling cot
sitting up at each entrance,
standing keenly over you
as they change your midnight IV –
I pray, too, that I may accept
the rest of the mother-bear's knowledge,
the part that knows
at some point you must
run off ahead of me
on your own.

JAMES MCGRATH

SOMETIMES I THINK OF THE DEATH
THAT HAS NOT HAPPENED YET

Sometimes I think about the death
        that has not happened yet.

It will come,
It will come,
        and I want to be ready to accept its gift,
        if there is one.

I want to be able
        to unwrap the thin coverings
        of memory upon memory
        agonizing on the joys,
        shrieking over the pains,
        trying to fill in the blanks
        where nothing happened,
        where everything stood still
            knee deep in swamp waters
            and pussy willows
            dripping with pollen.

I can not imagine
        the well of silence I will fall into.

I can not imagine
        what will be gone,
        what is not to be there
        when I reach out in the night
        to touch the soft age speckled hands
        and there is only emptiness.

And worse will be my wanting,
     pleading for deafness,
     because her voice
     has gone to where all echoes go...

     back to yesterday
     and into the mouths of fading faces
     in photographs.

KAREN ETHELSDATTAR

GENTLE THE SMALL RAIN

Gentle
the small rain
the mist hanging tenderly
over & among the fallen, the falling leaves.

Perhaps it resulted from a minor stroke…
My father, in these days, no longer stern & certain,
is a kid let out of school,
repeating snatches of songs & poems
with the pride of a boy,
splashing them through the brilliant
drifts of leaves,
skipping them like stones across the water
of brooks soon to be stilled with the thin film of winter.

He washes dishes
& dries Mother's back after a bath
in her last days
as he might once have carried
his first girl's schoolbooks,
off-handedly.
Their touching is clumsy, tentative,
mysterious as a first kiss.
Almost, they need a go-between.
What was taken for granted
is new each moment, important & unimportant.
Sharp words have disappeared like last year's leaves.
This year's words are gold as this season's leaves,

have the aroma of Valencia oranges
in their sweetness.
Silences between are the places on branches sealing over
where the leaves just let go.

My father is like a kid let out of school.
And Mother's death, perhaps, will be that way, too.

JANE ROHRER

TRANSITION

Three days ago
I was concerned
because he sat up in bed,
Over and over,
Leaned forward toward me and said,
"How will we get out of here?"
"How can I get out of here?"
"Can we go now?"

Now he doesn't speak,
doesn't sit,
only lies exhausted
in a twilight zone of consciousness
nested in the bed,
having found the answer.

LINDA VAUGHAN

LEGACY

An honor guard
of wind and rain
pays him tribute
while three children
with stunned blue eyes
wonder, where is Papa?

An old man can see again,
looks tenderly
at his wife's sweet dumpling face,
keeps a sharp eye on his cronies
at the Saturday afternoon card game,
savors a solitary neighborhood stroll
to inspect his world.

In the autumn light of a Nebraska dawn,
a dying man is given life,
will cradle his newborn grandson,
greet moonlit prairie nights,
gaze astonished into
his wife's grateful eyes.

On the Eastern shore,
a woman's life ebbs like tide
through salt marshes,
comes flooding back,
she will read cherished books,
drink tea with lifelong friends,
give thanks daily.

DEMENTIA

BARRY BALLARD

HIS REARRANGEMENT OF ROOM

He created a wide space for his last
conversations (swept clean from losing his wife
to Alzheimer's). And I took a childlike
risk and entered that pitch black room that passed
rest and unrest for something in-between.
There were muffled tremors while I waited
for my eyes to adjust, for one small thread
of shape that could answer that silent scream

of questions he kept hiding in his face.
But there never were answers to explain,
or truth in the accidents of wordplay.
Just the distinct sound of the folded brace
and leg of a hospital bed, the pain
of no sound when she finally slipped away.

JANE ROHRER

TIME

I come in February,
remove the Christmas crèche from outside her door,
replace it with the seasonless cornhusk doll and painted bell.
Put away the porcelain Christmas tree with tiny electric lights,
take down the quilted holly wall hanging,
change the calendar from January to February,
continue the pretense that the passing of time
is noticed
in my mother's world.

ROBERT WATERS GREY

TRIPLE DIGITS

When Mary arrived
light ricocheted off
the walls all over you.
Headlocked, hammerlocked,
body slammed, pinned flat
to the mattress, too weak
to raise a hand against it,
you were unable to fathom
defeat, so the silent
countdown continued.

The morning nurse,
Comfort, would have
blocked the blinding
rush, had she not been
sent home, sapped by fever.
Used to the graveyard shift,
yet wholly opposed to gloom
at any hour, her substitute,
Mary, having instinctively
flicked on the switch which
spewed a ghostly sheen upon
your deteriorating physique,
escorted us out, in order
to do to you whatever her
supervisors had planned.

Resigned to visits
which would never be

better than bad at best,
we stifled festering rage
and kept our peace, then,
as always, standing by,
marking time, on call.

Your early days of bitter
confusion at the nursing
home had swollen into six
years of incoherent absence.
Eight was the given mean for
survival after the onset of
Alzheimer's, but many hung
on for twenty. Due to your
naturally quirky nature, we
were blind to initial signs
of the brain's degeneration.
Further diverted and lulled
by the outwardly static yet
quick decline, we did not
expect an apparent end
at any specific time.

"I really miss your mother,"
remarked the arts and crafts
director, when you no longer
sang and danced with the rest
or tried to color within lines,
and a host of caretakers, still
amazed at your native strength,
praised you highly for fighting
their honest, but poor attempts
to comfort and care for you.

Once the disease had cataracted
your body light-years away from
its dogged spirit, you often lay
strapped against a tilted chair
stationed in the corridor, where
you favored a partially swathed
mummy with eyes already sounding
the next level. Within earshot,
madly gesticulating and shaking
their heads, workers reminisced
about earlier days of captivity
when, fresh off the sheep farm,
you tried to escape by slugging
a brawny nurse in the face and
clambering over the chain link
fence, then deadened your flesh
to endless care by resurrecting
yourself as a timeless wanderer
chosen to rearrange the home's
supplies, aggravate nosy old
women, and dare to corrupt
the most well-preserved
octogenarian men.

Because the flickering
spirit, even with most
of the brain disabled,
was still tied to your
body shutting down, we
travelled for hours to
visit, or witness when
you were not responsive,

needing to connect for
an awkward moment with
whatever inside us
was ill-prepared
to let go.

Although opposed
to gratuitous pain,
we never thought to
rush the ugly affair.
With emotions gutted
in order to spare our
feelings, we even mused
that if you slogged on
for another eleven years,
the President would send
official congratulations.
Bedridden with her stroke
for fourteen years, your
own mother remained lucid
close to the end, but died
five years shy of a century.
Years earlier, after I had
wished aloud that she would
reach one hundred, you had
paled and sighed, "I hope
not." Now, I understand.

When we dropped by
three months before
Mary's arrival scorched
the room, you were calmer
and lighter, as if yielding

to the caustic forces beyond
your control, but reluctant
to let you leave that easily,
doctors rewarded your flesh,
which clung like a hidebound
curse, for its backbone, by
offering coumadin to prevent
another stroke, even though
your brain seldom urged your
limbs to stir or told your
tongue to fashion sounds
which mimicked words.

Before Mary spun into
the room like a fireball
slinging convulsive light,
you were cold to the touch,
yet consumed by a white heat
from being forsaken by time
which kept you alive. Headed
home through a driving silence,
we brooded upon the measureless
stretch through which you would
have to endure what you could not
withstand, as others counted down.

Nine days later,
we learned your
body and spirit
had made up their
minds to reunite,
and suddenly all
of the numbers
stopped.

James McGrath

Remains
for Millie

It is not in my birth
       that my mother found her voice

I will not pray for a longer life for her
She is 93 with four years of dementia.

She has outlived her two brothers,
       and Minnie and Alma.

She has kept the blackberry stains
      on her lips,
      the thorns in her fingers.

She planted her gentleness
      among iris and trilliums
      for 70 years.

She trimmed her camellia bush
      and swept up the tears
      of red petals week after week
      blotting out the sun.

I've kept her scorched brown cookie sheets.
They hold her hand prints.

I've kept her piecework quilts
      with the torn edges.
      They warm the bits of childhood I retain.

I've kept the silver wedding coffee maker
        with the ivory handle,
        the tray, the sugar and creamer.
        They pour out the lady that
        she tries to hold onto.

I've kept the cut glass pitcher of her mother
        sharp edged and flowered.

I will not pray for a longer life for her.

Her world lies scattered about
        in the corners of my home
        and on the streets of South Tacoma
        where the stones from her garden
        paved the potholes of our family life.

I am uncertain what will remain
        of my mother when she leaves.

I do pray she will go like the camellia petals.

I do hope she will carry her secrets away
        without leaving any notes
        or telephone messages.

Her cat is gone.
The house is sold.
Her earrings wait for the granddaughters.

I will not pray for a longer life for my mother.

I want her to lie full of peace
        next to my father
        under the dogwood and holly.

I know she will speak her silence
        to me.

Then it may be the time to listen.

GRIEVING

CHARLOTTE G. ARNOLD

SATURDAY

With one or two
small exceptions –
there were
approximately
fifteen thousand
nine hundred and
thirty
seven
days
when I didn't miss you
like this.

Today
I miss you for all of them.

Holly Hagen

Going on When There's No Place to Go

Day One:

> The moment when all my eyes
> could wander up to
> were the flat plane of beeps;
> they nervously tracked the straight line,
> the straight back,
> the wedge
> that separated me from
> the conscious and the sane.
> The tape that tugged at each individual hair
> held under its restraint.

Day Five:

> My mom handed me a Teddy bear today
> with matted fur and a guardian angel pin
> and said, "Hug this whenever you
> feel sad."
> I hugged it so tightly that I passed out
> and when I awoke,
> I thought it had all been a dream.

Day Nine:

> I woke up this morning and gagged.
> My mom threw a pink bathrobe
> over the floor as I spewed blood
> and coughed mucus.
> My dad turned around and cried a tear
> out of the corner of his eye.

DAY TWENTY-THREE:
> I looked at my dad today
> and thought of how when you were little
> you thought your parents
> could fix anything.
> I looked at him and pleaded with my eyes,
> "Dad, why can't you fix this?"
> If he heard me ask this
> I knew he would've cried
> and I didn't want to go to sleep
> knowing that I had made my dad cry.

DAY SIXTY-SEVEN:
> I'm sitting in my shrink's office
> watching to where my pant cuffs
> trail off onto the floor.
> I always sit on the couch in the shrink's office.
> She asks me what I'm thinking
> and I'm thinking about her plants;
> about why hers grow and mine die.
> Instead of answering her,
> I laugh in her face.

DAY ONE HUNDRED AND TWO:
> I'm beginning to look at people and life
> in different ways
> and maybe, my mom says, I'll get better
> one day,
> but I can't see that far into the future
> so I'll just try to live for today.

DAY TWO HUNDRED AND FORTY-FOUR:
     I rearrange my bed so I can look
     out the window as I drift to sleep.
     I watch my plants grow as
     the clouds move over the grayish sky
     and think,
     "Is it the sky moving or is it
     the Earth?"

DAY THREE HUNDRED AND SIXTY-FIVE:
     I wake up at 2 a.m.
     and cry.
     I open the curtains and watch the stars
     and think about rotations.
     The stars disappear into
     pinks, purples and oranges.
     When I get up everyone looks at me like
     I'm going to have a mental breakdown
     and all I thought was,
     "My God, I'm twenty."

BILL BROWN

BURYING THE DEAD

I stare out the kitchen window
into that blank screen
and resurrect my brother
so that I can bury him again.
And I want to know why
some people make such a dent
with their short lives
that they can't stay dead,
and how many times can
a person be dug up and buried
before they can rest.

It's like the onion theory in theater.
Take one of Chekhov's characters,
peel off a layer of skin and there's
another complication of emotions
waiting underneath. You keep peeling,
finding new ones until nothing's left
but skinned layers on the floor,
and a small empty space from the center,
which dissipates into thin air.

When you raise the vision of the dead
so many times, feelings must be lost.
Maybe that's how we love and grieve people
until the love and the grief are just
half opaque emotions scattered about
our flesh, buried beneath layers of skin,
dispersed in tiny molecules

among the texture of our cells,
pumping with the blood through our hearts,
until that little empty space is just there,
something missed fondly
like the hopeful loneliness we wake to
when words can't explain our dreams.

ESTELLE PADAWER

DIRGE

Each morning your death
hangs like weights
on the ends of my lips
leaving just enough space
for gray moans to slip out
and drop all around me

littering my landscape
in mournful monotony.
This dreary dirge lightens a little
as the hands of the clock
reach up to pray

But their prayers lose potency
as they wind down the night
Like a fugue it chases me endlessly
I have no place to flee.

Giovanni Malito

In the Woods

Along the trail
a beaten path
he further pounds
into a deeper rut
he looks
from side to side
for a squirrel,
a bird,
a distraction

But he sees
only the front
of his mind
where she lives
and will not die
so he takes her
and walks along
arm in arm
out of himself.

LIZ CROW

A CERTAIN KNOWING

So this is grief.
When hearts wrench and senses numb
tears make salt-water truth.
And in the long spaces, birdsong cheats the silence
and affronts the soul.

ANGER

SHANNON SEXTON

MOTHER EULOGY

I.

It began
as a small storm,
a small lump
under the armpit.

The doctor said, nothing wrong. Healthy
as an apple.
Thirty-nine
is too young anyway.

II.

Trading Merry Christmas for *fuck you*
for the first time in her life,
she said *fuck you* to the pain
rippling through her
like an explosion.
To her husband,
working late hours,
avoiding visits
and cracking jokes.
To the gynecologist
who told her
the lump in her breast
was not malignant.
To the mammogram
that reinforced his deadly diagnosis.

III.

Nine months later,
her struggle spread out
like bedsheets—
bald head, swollen
breast, fat
fingers clasping the other hand,
are twice its size.

In her final weeks, a woman,
throwing fists
in the eye of a storm.

IV.

The doctors said two years
but they lied. They lied.

It takes so much
to kill a mother.

PAMELA USCHUK

THE JITTERING WIND
for Ella

Who is the wind jittering the top of Salt Cedars limbs,
shaking white eggs from the Mockingbird's nest?

Today, again in the emergency room
my mother responsive as an unlit candle
to a dark room, her blood pressure
barely ticking, I sat beside her bed,
reading by the light of the oxygen hiss, the split
green beeps of the heart monitor, pouring
over text, trying to learn
the one Russian word for health.

Who is the wind flicking empty pods
burst from the Mexican Bird of Paradise
that blocks our back door?

What hand in the ice-singed light of the trauma ward
would pull the warm blanket around
my mother's neck, if I didn't stay,
if I went home, wasted after another day
waiting for doctors' decisions to solve her grief.

Who is the wind that drifts pollen into our eyes
so we cannot see the way we'd travel?

I am so tired of dying. The past four years
my mother has gone from wife to widow to spasming infant.
One Doc says she's hydrocephalic, should have

a shunt cut into her seventy-eight year old skull.
Another says nonspecific neurological disorder.
Nonspecific. What bastard will cut the pole
on which to display her amputated head?
I am sick of death's choking asphalt,
the long exhaustion of brain ventricles
that stop working one by one.

Mama, who is the wind and how much
does it demand for your ransom?

Zyskandar A. Jaimot

I Heard My Mother Sentenced to Die...

from a man of ethical profession
        who was not my father
in a hospital hallway
        where blood is never allowed or seen
because blood
        is associated with suffering
and there is no suffering here
        because it is overcome
by clouds of ammonia disinfectant
        where nurses with needles
inject mindlessness on demand to ease you into anterooms
        of death certificates waiting to be filled out
by supposed healers
        hiding behind gauze masks
in this special place
        where my mother was sentenced to die
so matter of factly
        by a man who was a surgeon
who would see none of my mother's tears
        when she would stare in a mirror
touching the puckered purple skin
        where mastectomy scars would never heal
and no one would ever see
        as her fingers traced memories
in breathless moments of warm lips
        that had vanished with the cold stainless touch
from a stranger slicing away her life's supposed beauty
        breasts removed by a man
with words that strangle all hope

in the malignancy of existence
and I heard my mother sentenced to die
from a man of ethical profession
who never witnessed my father's face
while he lifted my embarrassed mother
into his arms from off the foul-stained bedsheets
no longer able to control herself
in that phase of remission as transient as day-lilies
while we stood around in hushed reverence
as if we were already in some church at prayer
hearing only my father's voice of helplessness
swearing to us that cancer
is now a tarot-card of recurring curse
and I heard my mother sentenced to die
from a man of supposed compassion who never asked
why she always felt so cold
and never saw the sweater she always wore
even in the yellowing of summer
as we watched her shrivel
from the chemicals and radiation
into the bald hollows of her dull eyes
which never saw
my father's dim reflection ever after
in a mirror where his fingers rubbed
over-and-over touching that sore place
as if he could bring back breathless moments
long after the final passion.

MARIANNE POLOSKEY

THE CHAIRS IN THE GARDEN
OF THE NURSING HOME

First time we looked at the place
the garden was neat,
like a room straightened
for company. Even the residents
had been swept back
inside the house. We saw
what we needed to see:
roses rounding out summer,
lawns soaking up shade of trees
so tall they were above pain.
Later, when she was living there,
we saw the chairs,
scattered as for a party,
restraining the bounce of grass.
Stiff chairs hostile
to my mother's back, to which
she yielded as she yielded
to everything else,
for what choice did she have.
Orange plastic chairs
that marred the garden
where we sat in silence
through diminishing afternoons.
Chairs in which she cried
more often during the two weeks
of my visit than she had
ever cried before. Wobbly chairs
against which we steadied

each other by holding hands,
unable to let go.
I came to hate those chairs
in which she looked so alone.
Hated them like parting.
Like the flimsiness
of life.

WIDOWHOOD

Rogan Wolf

The Widow

She wears two wedding rings these days.
That single wracked finger
eighty years in the making
is now all that holds her marriage together.

She can't conceive what's happened to her.
Some god broke into that dim flat of theirs
and in a swirl of white moments fished away
her world's heart, her whole history.

She sits at the end of our settee
all scrunched up as the clock keeps beating
out the time. Each emerging moment
just disgorges more pain. Her dead has it easy.

She remembers the funeral. She shrieked to him then:
"My eyes!
     My *eyes*!
          Where *are* you?
               I'm *blind*!"
And she grabs at that finger and those sweet lips
cover her rings with frantic abandon.

Mary H. Eastham

What He Left

We had returned to our courting days. Talking. Holding hands. "What will make a difference in all of this," Paul said to me just days before he died, "is how I loved you." At the funeral I wanted to get into the coffin with him. Close the cover down over our faces. I could die quickly.

An alarm goes off somewhere in the house. A reminder for my Paul to take his pain pill. The neurosurgeon looked straight at Paul when he said, "You might want to get your things in order." He spent the next hour with us. He was always there to answer my questions and yet what I remember most about him was the awful truth of that one sentence he had committed to memory.

The doorbell rings. I walk through empty space like a ballerina, my eyes fixated on one small point straight ahead, the stem of a four-leaf clover on the wallpaper in the kitchen, the sober burgundy stain that rises above the pale white trim on the walls of the study. I don't let the haunted corners of the rooms draw me close. At the full length mirror in the front hall, I touch my fingers to the glass. I realize I haven't changed my dress for two days.

When I open the door a young woman says, "I'm Gloria from Benson Kennels." She looks weary. She lowers her eyes as she continues. "Your husband arranged this for you. Before…" She is still talking, but I only see her lips moving. She places a golden retriever puppy in my arms. Attached to his collar is a postcard, one Paul and I found together, an artist's sketch of Paris just before nightfall. In the picture, a woman is standing on the curb of a busy street, her small dog standing beside her. It looks like she is waving to someone. Paul said it reminded him of me greeting him when he came home from a trip. We both loved the vibrance of the sky, the way the fuchsia sunset made us feel. "Electrified, so full of life" was the phrase I think Paul used. The puppy squirms as I turn the card over and read my husband's last message to me—"Love him for both of us—Paul."

I put the puppy down on the floor. In a quiet daze, I follow him into the kitchen where for just a moment I can pretend the last few days never happened. As the puppy and I form circles around one another, I am reminded of another time when we were living in a tiny studio apartment. It was raining. We had no money. Paul serenaded me with his one man kitchen-counter-top-sound, which was really a frying pan turned upside down and two spoons, while I twirled around in the middle of the floor, careful not to knock anything over.

What am I doing? Tired, I stop. The puppy, not yet ten weeks old, continues to chase his tail, or a scent, or nothing in particular, his tiny blonde footsteps forming invisible tracks in the grooves of the wood, tracks he will come back to tomorrow and the next day, and the day after that, whenever he needs to find something familiar.

The porch light goes on. "Paul?" I say. The puppy runs to the window, hoisting himself up against the wooden ledge. I press his small body into the arc of my arms. Folded into one another near the open window, we are like two butterflies setting out on our first mission, fearful of the night sounds that will one day guide us. In the distance there is a pop, like something on fire, something electrified. The puppy looks up at me, his eyes like tiny candles lit from within. I tell him not to worry, that somewhere out there beyond the bruised evening sky, in the wide mouth of the unknown, a star releases its energy into the night.

MARLEE MILLMAN

WIDOWHOOD: JOURNEY THROUGH A CLOSED DOOR

"...Grief is a train that doesn't run on anyone
else's schedule...Hearts heal faster from surgery
than from loss. And when the center of someone's
life has been blown out...is it any wonder if it
takes so long even to find a door to close?"
                                        Ellen Goodman

I am lying in bed…it's not my bed. It's my nephew's bed. I am staying at my sister's house. It's the morning after the day of the funeral. I can't move. My legs and arms feel paralyzed and my stomach burns like paper in a fireplace.

I have just buried my husband.

When I open my eyes, my sister, Janice, is standing there. She touches my arm and asks how I am doing. All I can do is look up at her with tears streaming down my face and say, "I don't know what I am going to do." I can't imagine how I am ever going to get out of bed, let alone begin my life again. I think it's a nightmare from which I will awaken and Ron will be here. But Ron will never be here.

I finally get out of bed and drag myself to the bathroom. I know there are people coming by to offer their condolences, and I have to be there to greet them. I don't want to talk to anyone. I don't want to put on a courageous face. I am expected to be a hostess, when I can hardly lift my head let alone engage in conversation. It would be much better to have this mourning period occur a month or two after the funeral; maybe then I would more than welcome company.

"Oh my dear, how awful for you. How did it happen?"
"Wasn't there anything anyone could do?"

"Were you there when he died?"

"How long was he sick?"

"I hope he didn't suffer."

"You should get a job. It will be good for you."

And, on and on and on. My head is spinning and my eyes feel as if they are bulging out of my sockets. When one group leaves, another comes.

I am watching an awful movie that won't end.

After two days and two nights, the flow of people stops. The condolence period is officially over and I am faced with a life turned upside down.

I am spiraling downward like Alice, and I'm not going to end up in any Wonderland. I know I can't stay at Janice's house forever, although I sure want to. A week goes by; she and I sit at the table in her sunlit kitchen with windows that overlook a ravine filled with large oak trees. We have just finished breakfast and the empty cereal bowls are piled at the end of the table.

Janice reaches across the table and takes both of my hands in hers. "I think we have to talk about your going home," she says.

I have been thinking about that also, but I didn't want to raise the subject.

"The longer you stay, the more difficult it will be for you," she continues.

"I know," I say. "Oh God, Jan, I never dreamed this would happen."

She gets up from her chair and comes over and gives me a hug. "Neither did I," she says and starts to cry. Now I am comforting her instead of the other way around.

****

Janice and my good friend Carole drive me back to my apartment and when we arrive at my building the doorman comes out to help with the suitcase I had taken to my sister's. "I am so sorry for your loss," he says. "Mr. Millman was such a nice man."

"Thank you," I say and we all walk through the lobby to the mailbox, where I pick up all the mail that's been stored for me. I know my legs are moving, but they might as well be on someone else's body. I know my purse is on my shoulder, but it could be hanging on a coat rack. I am in a fog as if I am looking through a large piece of white gauze. We take the elevator up to my apartment and walk in the front door. I stand in the middle of the living room looking around, I feel like I am seeing my apartment for the first time. The wall unit containing the television set is in front of me; the two rose-colored reclining chairs are behind me; the mauve glass-encased credenza is to my right and the bookshelves to my left. They are there as they always are, but the setting looks different. Of course, it's different. I am now living without Ron.

Janice and Carole stand in the hall leading to the living room. I walk over to them, kiss them good-bye and close the door behind them. Oh my God, I think, I can't do this. I turn around to open the door and call after them to take me back, but I stop. I know I have to stay. I press my body against the door and slowly slide to the floor. I sit with my arms wrapped around my bent legs and my head lying on my knees. I am not sure how long I sit in this position, but eventually I walk back into the living room. My entire body is trembling, and I collapse into my rose-colored "womb" chair. The rest of the evening is a big blur.

****

I am not sure how I survive the next days, weeks, months and even years. I greet the day saying "shit" and feel the butterflies in my stomach. I always get up though, take a shower and get dressed. I think that by doing the things I always did, I can override the pain and the depression. It doesn't happen that way, but it is important for me to continue my routine. Most of the time, after I perform these tasks, I sit in my "womb" chair and stare into space or put on the television and stare into the screen. I need to have voices in the background. I can't stand the incessantly loud silence.

For the first three weeks, I cannot leave the house. I can't get the mail, as that means taking an elevator to the lobby. I don't want to talk to people who are just neighbors. I don't want to smile and say "good morning" or "hello, how are you." I don't want to respond to "how are you doing?" I can barely talk and when I do, I start to cry.

My mother, sister and friends come over and bring me food, although I can't eat. I try to read, but I can't concentrate. When the reality of my living without Ron creeps in, I start to shake and my stomach cramps. I think that if I take a walk when these thoughts enter my head, it will ease the pain… But I can't leave the house. I can't get myself out of the malaise of mourning. I'm afraid if I leave the house; I won't be able to get back.

I start to write in a journal. I read that writing can be therapeutic. These entries are filled with anger. I write the same thing over and over…. *Life is cruel…I miss Ron so…it will never be the same…why did this happen…I'm being punished…I feel awful…why should I go on living…what do I have to live for…why does life have to be so hard…I'm so lonely…will these feelings ever leave…will I ever recover…*And, I cry and cry.

The desire to see Ron is so powerful that it finally gets me out of the house. I need to see him and the only thing that gives me comfort is visiting the cemetery. I go on a Saturday when I know no one will be around and just sit and talk to him. Other times I walk to the beach and sit on the pier and talk to him there. I have to hold on to him. Many times I open his closet and bury my head in his clothes. I don't want to get rid of anything of his. I find a sweatshirt that he wore in the hospital and I wear it a lot.

****

Four months into the grieving, I begin to have sexual stirrings. What is this? I think, is this normal? My heart starts to pound and I feel tingling all over. I thought the sexual part of me was dead. I call a friend whose husband died five years prior. "Jane,

I hope I don't embarrass you with this question, but you are the only one I can ask," I say. "Did you feel horny around four months after Jack died?" "Um," she says. "You know I went to this party a few nights ago and Nancy's husband asked me how I am doing without a man. Can you imagine that? He's such a jerk." "That's not what I am asking, Jane," I say and repeat the question. She evades the question again and I stop asking. That's when I start to haunt book stores and the library to find something that will tell me that everything I am feeling is normal. I don't want to read statistics on how there are more widows than widowers. I don't want to read about how I should volunteer my time because it will make me feel better and enhance my self-esteem. I don't want to read that a "new sense of inner strength develops through suffering."

I want to read what happened is the worst thing that can happen to a person. I want to read that whatever I am feeling, be it depression, anger, shock, pain, desire, is normal. I want to read someone else's journey. I want to know if the pain ever lifts and if there is a timetable for it.

****

I am 51 at the time of Ron's death and think I want to meet women or men close to my age who are going through what I am. People with whom I can share the daily ups and downs: the waking up at 3:00 a.m. and realizing I am sleeping alone; wanting to die; the breakthrough of not thinking about Ron every minute of the day; the desire to have another relationship and the always-present feeling that widowhood sucks. But I realize I am too selfish and don't want to hear anyone else's pain. I also think that I will only find groups of older people whose agendas are much different from mine. They will probably have children and grandchildren, and been married 40 years or more. I do not fit in either category. I have no children and was married for 12 years. So I never try very hard to find a support group and I will never know if one would have helped. I endure the best I can with the help of my sister, a few good friends and my therapist.

****

Some say the first year of widowhood is the hardest, but I disagree. It gets more difficult as the years pass and it's been nine years since Ron died. When the shock wears off and the pain disappears, I am still left with the reality of going it alone.

There is no one to wake up with and say "good morning."

There is no one to share the daily events of life.

There is no one to turn to and say, "How about a movie tonight?"

There is no one to hug and kiss intensely.

The worst part of widowhood is the finality. I will never see Ron again.

I miss him more today than the day he died.

MARK BLICKLEY

THE PIGEON MAN SINGS

It's freezing outside. I'd say my fingers feel like icicles but the truth is I can't feel them at all, they're so numb. I've tried to toss the popcorn with my gloves on but it doesn't work. You can't aim. It always falls to the ground in a clump and that means the stronger and greedier pigeons crowd out the weaker ones.

My name's Wendell Mandanay and though I've lived in this neighborhood for nearly seventy years, most folks know me as the Pigeon Man. Kids sometimes taunt me. They shout 'Pigeon Man! Pigeon Man!' like it was something I should be ashamed of. But I don't really think they mean any harm. They're just bored, that's all, though I do get upset when they throw stones at the birds.

I've been feeding pigeons for eighteen years. I try not to miss a day. Sometimes my shoulder acts up, starts really hurting, and it's too painful to even put my coat on. That's when the pigeons miss a meal. Those kind of days seem to be more frequent lately and I feel bad for the birds.

My shoulder problems come from forty years of carrying a mail sack for this city. I'm not complaining. I enjoyed being a mailman when I handed folks a letter that made them smile. Some days my letters made them cry. When I was a younger letter carrier that used to bother me, but as I got older I realized bad news traveling through the mail is kind of like the weather – sometimes you can predict it but you can never change it.

Three months ago I moved into the Senior Citizen Housing the city opened last year. It's okay. The rent's real cheap and it is closer to the park. Up until now I've ignored all the group activities the Senior Commission have organized. Mostly they've been bingo games and chartered buses to the casinos at Atlantic City.

I'm not a gambling man. Heck, I'd never have bet I'd live as long as I have. And what were the odds that me, Wendell

Mandanay, twelve years older than my wife, Anna, would outlive her by eighteen years? Do you know that after dozens of years of living with that woman the thing I miss most about her is her smile.

Lately the days seem to be getting darker quicker and I'm not so sure it's because of winter. That's why I've decided to tell a secret I've kept for nearly twenty years.

The day after I buried my wife I stopped eating. I didn't plan to stop feeding myself; it just happened. I enjoyed the taste of certain foods and had earned considerable praise for my cooking skills, but now the only taste I desired was beer. And plenty of it. All I had to do was pick up the phone and thirty minutes later there'd be a case of it outside my door.

When Anna was alive we enjoyed taking walks and enter-taining in our home. But these days I kept close company with the television set. I'd spend most of the time laying on the couch, sipping beer and listening to the T.V. The television talked at me day and night. Sometimes I'd awaken in the morning or the afternoon or at night and to my surprise recall the exact content of programs overheard in my sleep.

The neighbors grew concerned. Every couple of days it seemed someone would knock on my door. I'd rouse myself from the couch, place the beer bottles on the floor beneath the coffee table and quietly answer the door.

"Good afternoon, Wendell."

"It is a fine afternoon."

"How are things going, Wendell?"

"I'd say about three hundred and sixty degrees."

"Is there anything I can get you, Wendell?"

"As a matter of fact, there is."

"What is it, Wendell? What do you need?"

"I could use a smile. Whenever I answer a knock I never see one. Everybody always looks so upset, so nervous."

"That's because we're worried about you, Wendell."

"But it's all the unhappy faces at my door that make me worry."

"If I can be of an assistance, Wendell, you know where to find me."

"Thank you. But to find you would mean that I lost you and I hope our friendship never comes to that. Good afternoon."

I just wanted to be left alone. When Anna died not only did I lose my appetite, but I stopped cleaning up our apartment. And then I stopped cleaning myself.

About a month or so after my wife's funeral I was watching a nature show on Public Television. It was about pigeons. I was asleep, a little groggy, and didn't pay much attention. Not too much sunk in. Or so I thought.

When I woke up the next morning (or a few hours later) and went to the fridge for a beer, I kept hearing the narrator's voice in my head. He was telling me things like:

'Pigeons usually mate for life, rearing squabs season after season, often for ten years or longer.'

'All pigeons naturally love to bathe and to keep their feathers clean and shining.'

'Pigeons do not overeat.'

'Mated pigeons are generally more productive if the male is decidedly older than the female.'

I thought it was strange remembering that program because I always hated pigeons. To me they were nothing more than flying rats. And let me tell you, they made my life miserable when I was a mailman.

I quickly forgot about the birds when I discovered I was down to my last three bottles of beer. When I phoned the corner liquor store they refused to deliver. I owed them money from the last bill.

This meant I had to go out to get it. And going outside was the last thing I wanted to do. I didn't want to get cleaned and dressed, yet I didn't want people to see me like that. So I compromised by taking a shave and hiding the rest of myself under a hat and an overcoat Anna had dry-cleaned for me. It was still in its plastic bag.

After pouring two bottles of beer down my throat I closed the door behind me. On the way to the liquor store I saw a huge flock of pigeons. Some wretch had dumped bags of garbage in front of my building and the birds were having a feast.

They were all gobbling up that garbage except for this one bird. He had his back to the food and looked like he was tucked real tight inside his feathers. I walked around to face him.

I wasn't in front of him more than two seconds when he lifts his beak and stares up at my face. I got such a chill looking at his eyes, and this was in the middle of August. I tried to walk away but couldn't. The pigeon wouldn't let me go.

That's when I realize the bird wasn't eating because he'd lost his mate. So I kneeled down, a bit unsteady from the beer I'd just drunk and the heavy overcoat, and gave him a pep talk. I told him to stop feeling sorry for himself, to stop punishing himself because his wife would hate to see him like that. I whispered that his wife had a husband she could respect and it was unfair to her memory if he became a bird that couldn't be respected.

And don't you know the pigeon starts bobbing his head like he's agreeing with me. So I stood up and hurried over to the grocery store for some birdseed. When I returned he was gone. The other birds were still pecking at the garbage, but my pigeon had disappeared.

Being out in the fresh air must've made me hungry. That night I cooked myself a big supper. The next day I began to feed the pigeons, just in case my bird was part of a hungry flock.

Susan Taylor

Waving Goodbye, Waving Hello

Emily would be home from college soon, and she would have to explain. The question was how. How to tell her daughter everything, in a way that Emily wouldn't reject, interrupt, tell her what her own words really meant. Agnes looked down at the surface of the kitchen table. It was cluttered with dishes there was no room for in the sink and this week's newspapers. Her new cat, Cat, had plopped himself smugly in the center of the newspapers. What her husband had always said about cats was true, she had to admit, but now she found herself delighting in Cat's bad tendencies: he jumped up on things, shed hair everywhere and once she had caught him on the table, licking the butter. Now he was on the newspapers, extending a paw toward her dinner plate.

"Oh, you big fat thing," she told him. He looked up at her with honey gold eyes and yawned. There was a tablet of note paper on the table, each piece had a photograph of the realtor who had sent it, along with a magnet with his face and telephone number and a letter informing her that after bereavement many people find their houses too large, too much to maintain on their own, and he would be happy to provide her with a free market estimate and representation if she wanted to sell her home. She had thrown the magnet away, but had kept the note pad because paper is always useful. Now she took the pen she used for writing grocery lists and tapped its point thoughtfully against the realtor's face. Maybe a note, something Emily would have to read.

> *I'm at my Grief Group tonight.*
> *I want to explain about what you'll find in the backyard.*
> *I want to tell you about your father.*

If I'd known, I would have had you come home. But it was too much to ask you to just come home for the funeral.
The cat's name is Cat.

She frowned. A list wouldn't explain anything. She tore the page off and ripped it up. Cat batted at the scraps with a chubby velvet paw and then batted at the pen in her hand. She would just write it like she would say it, if Emily were listening.

Dear Emily,
I'm at my Grief Group tonight. I'm sorry I wasn't home when you got here, but it is very important to go every time. We are all widows except for one man, who lost his wife two months ago, and we depend on each other to be there. Tonight I am bringing dessert: instead of baking something I am walking to the store and getting ice cream. Since you father died I have begun walking everywhere or taking the bus for long trips. He always drove, you remember, because it made me too nervous.

She was out of room already. She folded the first page over the back of the pad and continued.

I like walking. I never did it much before but now I have my routes that I go on, and people say hello to me. I bundle up good and I'm careful on the ice. There is so much I never noticed before!

This wasn't explaining anything. She'd better get to the point, as Emily was always asking her to do.

It was on one of my walks that I got the idea for what's in the backyard. I was inching along over the icy sidewalk and I saw a glove lying on the snow.

How to explain how that glove, lying alone on its white bed, palm open and fingers outstretched, had spoken to her, had seemed to be in her same situation, how she'd leaned down and snatched it up and carried it home because it had seemed important. How could she explain to Emily that someone's lost glove was important?

I picked it up and then whenever I was on a walk, I seemed to find another one: never a pair, always just one lost glove. I took them all home and kept them in your father's empty t-shirt drawer, until it got hard to shut it... By March, all his drawers were full. I had to think of something else.

Wait. Emily wouldn't care about the gloves so much. First she should tell her about her father. That was what was important, and why she hadn't told her to come home.

I didn't think your father was all that sick. He never told me he felt bad, and you know how stubborn he was about going to the doctor. I should have known but I didn't... I just thought every day was the same, that nothing was changing. And that night when I was washing the supper dishes and he asked me to come upstairs and lay down with him didn't seem any different from any other night. I told him I wanted to finish the dishes. When I came upstairs he was already dead. Emily, I think of that now and I cry. There is no end to my crying, I cry oceans and the ache of it is too big for my chest. Honey, I am so sorry that I didn't know, I would have had you come home. If I had known.

If she had known, she would never have done the dishes. She would have taken him to the emergency room. They would have saved him. He would be here now, dozing in front of the television and she wouldn't be writing this note.

She folded the second page over the tablet and faced the third empty page.

I found Cat on one of my walks through the neighborhood. He popped out of a dumpster and frightened me. He was so skinny and dirty! As you can see, he's now huge and his fur is beautiful. I mix an egg and oil into his food to make him shiny. He followed me and kept mewing, so I had to pick him up. I didn't intend to keep him. We never had cats. Your father didn't like them. But Cat just decided I was his. He likes to be stroked under his chin. Try it. If it's nine and I'm not home yet, please let him out into the yard.

The yard.

What you will find in the yard is what I did with all the gloves. I had about a hundred of them, and none of them matched. How is that possible? They must make so many different kinds. The world never ceases to make me wonder. Well, I was looking at them filling up your father's bureau and then I happened to go outside and see our tree, with its branches all bare. I put the gloves into boxes and dragged them out there, found your father's old ladder and began hanging them from every little branch. I covered the tree with them, as far as I could reach from the ladder. They hang there like strange leaves.

The gloves touched her inside somehow, each hanging alone on a branch, all of them swinging in the wind. The tree looked so full now, the gloves all waving together.

When the wind blows, the gloves wave together, like they're waving good-bye, then waving hello.

Well, that was it, what she really wanted Emily to know. She pulled all the pages off the tablet and left them on the table for her daughter to find.

HOSPICE AND PALLIATIVE CARE

Richard Hain

St. Christopher's Hospice

My breath is etched in crystal smudges,
on the sharp blue air outside
and dry brown leaves crunch crisply under me.

And I'm treading a hushed hallelujah in the leaves
as my heart rejoices in the soft bronze warmth
mantling St. Christopher's; quiet brown, and halo-gold
where lives drop, gentle as the leaves
and whisper to their end
in a triumph of quietness.

RICHARD HAIN

BEGINNING

In water, my life began in white
in a deep snowstorm in a Kent village
while the doctor struggled to drive from home
and my father, still fresh and frightened
from the memory of blue babies
over whose birth he had been called to stand guard
watched, white-faced, until I cried.

There are many babies in my story.
They are laid like pearls along the line of my life,
warm and perfect in my palm,
but long ago one fell through my fingers and shattered,
and she had been the most perfect of all.

In the Spirit, my life began in black.
In a deep sadness, the summer I was sixteen.
By then I thought it my turn to stand guard
over other people's babies, and suddenly,
with horrifying gentleness, one slipped under my guard.
He lay in his pram like all the others who were only asleep,
but cool and white like broken chalk.

And this tore me, and ripped open a red gash in me
and through it, I fell out of the World
and started to fall in love.

CAROLYN BRIDGIT FLYNN

AMAZING GRACE

We have done this before.
Moistened the cloth
with warm water and soap,
wiped her body clean.
But then she moaned, and sighed,
and her arms did not
have this heaviness.

Still we sing the song.
Wash her hair, anoint her body with holy water
she herself brought from Ireland.
We wash her entire
her feet last, each part three times
and we hum the tune
while her skin is still warm and moist,
her face translucent.

Perhaps she has never looked more like herself
than in this final moment,
her spirit hovering above her earthly body.
The last creases of earthly care on her brow
smoothed to a fine glow.

Her priest says to pray for her easy travel
through the heavenly gates,
but I saw my mother's face
as she made that transition,
I saw her glow into the Great Heart
at the center of the world.

Final fluids rush from her body.
We wipe them clean, roll her to one side
then another. We touch her brow
like we are touching a holy relic.
We kiss her one last time
and watch them take her from us,
her face still glowing, even as
they zip cold plastic up to her neck,
even as they take her out the door
into bright sunlight. And we her children

watch her go, weeping, arms outstretched,
leaning together heavy inside the doorway
as though an invisible hand holds us,
and we are not meant to follow
into the brightness she is headed.

COMING TO PEACE

NOEL NOWOSIELSKI

DROWNING

Drowning in the deluge
of your own tears,
stormed by the man who use to
kiss your clouds;
These floods,
you proclaim,
Are a torrential disaster,
From which nothing,
not even the dam,
can be rebuilt.

But these waters will
subside—
They will;
And I will
find you
wallowing in the silten mud
of your own emotions,
waiting for your tears to dry
on the broken glass of hope's picture frame.

And dry they will;
Crystallize between the pane's cracks
amid the heat of his scorched photograph.
You want him to burn
Now as you
drown.

One day
your flame for him
will die;
Exhausted by its own heat,
Exalted by your moment's hate.

Droplets of his memory
will fall easier
before your eyes.

As the clouds rise
his mist will merely cast your horizon;
And his dew,
simply wake your mornings.

Suddenly,
one day,
your weather will be fine.
He will simply
find his place
in the lie of your land;
                    A little crease
                    in the history of your face;
                    A little line
                    in the hope of your hand.

CAROL MALLEY

BREATHING

I am standing in your space
between the calm of day
and the passion of night,
before the devastation of January,
the opaque despair of February,
the icy rage of March.

I am walking in the faded imprint
of your footsteps,
cold air kissing my cheeks raw,
wind combing my hair into disarray,
the frozen land holding me
as solidly as you once did,
as wholly as it now holds you.
I am breathing rich earth blackness,
trying to feel you in a gentler season.

BILL BROWN

THE SPRING AFTER YOUR DEATH

Late that afternoon
I watched from the kitchen window
as night erased the world.
Starting with the yard,
it washed the ground charcoal
until nothing was left
but the vague silhouette
of hickory limbs,
an intermittent choir of frogs,
and an abstract map inside
my chest I couldn't follow.

All night my heart,
that restless vagrant,
beat a path through
the maze of my ribs,
searching for something dear,
something lost in the tangled
ganglion of grief.

And in the morning
a soft mist lifted its veil
to blue and lavender phlox,
gathered in small congregations
beneath the stone wall of your garden,
like bright pilgrims on a one-time
journey to find what's holy.

Not suddenly, but as precious
as restful breath, something
deep inside my body canceled winter
and I strolled barefoot out
into the world
to find you gone.

RUTH DAIGON

SUDDEN AND STILL

Here to my hiding place bring me
succulents, honey bees, clover
to fill that vacant space,
lizards, wild flowers, shallots
to soften this brittle shell,
wine fire opal, ripening grain
to make me fertile again.

She slept so light
hardly an imprint on the sheet
and then she rose and slipped
away disturbing no one.
Now, like an eyelash caught
in a tear duct, I keep
blinking her back.

Again it's 4 A.M.
last night's wine stain
still on the table cloth,
moonlight coloring in
the shades of sleep.
Again the doorbell rings.
I filter the air before swallowing.

Which child is it?

But I know before knowing
and catch my breath
until the house is still
and I as motionless as she.

How long will my hand
cool in yours?

I keep ungluing memories
like snapshots, 3 x 5 moments,
carry her cubed in my palm,
turn my wrist to see
the infant, child, woman
and reach through her to lose myself.

I drape my life around me
like an old coat,
trace my patterns
through the house
and climb the stairs
until I reach the hovering place
where I can say

My eyes were steady enough
My body shelter enough
My right arm love enough.

ANN E. MICHAEL

MEDITERRANEAN DREAM
for m.

Last night, I dreamed you were living
in a Mediterranean town.
I walked from the sun-baked plaza
into a shaded alley
and found a terra-cotta courtyard
cool and empty.
The doors on every building
were oak and wrought iron;
it felt like a cathedral,
a town full of churches.

We had lunch on your small balcony
overlooking the valley,
red-tiled roofs
stretched out to the sea.
You would drink neither wine nor coffee.
You were thin and small,
wasting away
under shaded eaves
with the sun as bright as aching
and the sea a mirror beneath it.

We walked to a church;
one of those oaken doors
opened into it.
You clutched my arm, weakly,
you could not leave the pew
even to kneel. I kissed your head.

I watched you fade
into the dimness.

I prayed
I, who no longer believe
that God grants the wishes
of human beings,
I prayed you would be cured.
I prayed for your life
more fervently
than I have ever prayed
for anything. I woke
as that prayer broke open my grief
and sunlight sang through my body.

And you...I dreamed you were living.
In a Mediterranean town.

ALBERT HALEY

RED BALL

There was a wave far out, out in the ocean.
On the beach a man played with his family.
Out in the ocean, far out, the wave bore down.

The man's son tossed a red ball into the surf.
With joy and love and the best of everything
he had. But he wanted it back. The red ball.
Already. Come to me. "Daddy!" he shouted.

Not far out, out in the ocean, the wave
was coming, coming in. It was higher
than before. High. At least six feet high.

The man said, "I'll get it",
dove into the water like a slick arrow.

"Yes, Daddy!" The son's voice momentarily
louder than the ocean. He felt happy,
had not been happier that day.

Likewise the little girl who laughed
and danced in the sand.
Vacation time! Her brother.
Her mommy.
Her daddy.

The wave rose seven feet now.
It would exhaust stored energy
when it hit the shore
and then—

"No!" the man's wife said.
Waist deep in everything,
he looked at his family,
wife, son, daughter.

His hands lightly sculled.
He could not see except
what he wanted to see.
Thus he was able to smile.

The wet wall plowed over
and collapsed upon its cold
salty self.

(Such a phenomenon, arising without warning,
is called a "rogue wave."
No one knows what causes them,
no not exactly. An anomaly,
a massive pinching of the ocean
into a ridge moving fast
and fatal out of the flat safe blue,
overwhelming everything in its path.)

When the man washed ashore
they blew into his lungs.
He had returned, but it was not
a real homecoming. Only a body.
A slack container.
His head had struck rocky bottom

just as the last expiration of the wave
impressed itself above high tide mark

and left behind the skein of delicate foam.
Bubbles pop, pop.

And the ball?
It did not reappear.

Three days later they buried him.
"Freak accident," someone said.
"Death where is thy sting?" quoted the minister.

This is a true story.
And it has brought me a vision:

We are grains of sand clinging
to the shoreline. Intimately enfolded,
we wash back and forth.
We have our reprieve.
For now. Later we join the man
and those who have gone ahead.

Come that day these grains of sand
shall form a mountain.
And it is by faith that I think
I will find the tossed red ball
and hold it in my hand.

JOHN GREY

You Live in So Many Times

It's light and honed for travel
like a dream
but it really is just a thought.
It takes you back thirty years,
two thousand miles maybe.
You're on the patio of the hotel,
balancing a coffee in your hand.
You're staring out through the palm trees
at the sea.

My head is trying to keep you there
as long as possible.
It's like hands holding up your fatigued body,
placing that cup just so,
sketching in that blessed foreground
with all its primary colors,
its wind-shook shapes.

What I'm trying to tell you is
we live in all the moments,
not just this one.
You smile at me
and a halo rims your mouth.
Like much these days,
I look at it
like I'm remembering it.

Eulogies

Rogan Wolf

You Who Were Held

You who were held as a child
and as a lover
you we held in friendship in fellowship

you who were sister
and mother
you

you should be
with us here
on this edge.

It is unbelievable
it is unbearable
it is unacceptable

that you are not.
These outrageous shards
that fire has made of you

you wanted merged
with these gray coast-waters
full of your love and laughter.

It is only your love
we are left with now
as your ashes take to sea.

We shall never recover from the loss of you
but the absence we grieve for
is all love.

You leave behind
only benevolence.
Our world has been transformed

by you. You brought light.
It shall not go out.
Flesh you were

and flesh you are not
but the spirit you brought to the world
shall not leave it.

We are without you.
We are made of you.

ANNIE FINCH

VIGILS

In memory of Henry Leroy Finch, August 8, 1918-August 22, 1997

"Bequeath us to no earthly shore until
Is answered in the vortex of our grave
The seal's wide spindrift gaze towards paradise."
-Hart Crane, "Voyages"

"If a lion could talk, we couldn't understand it"
-Ludwig Wittgenstein

Under the ocean that stretches out wordlessly
past the long edge of the last human shore,
there are deep windows the waves have not opened,
where night is reflected through decades of glass.
There is the nursery, there is the nanny,
there are my father's magnificent eyes
turned towards the window. Is the child uneasy?
His is the death that is circling the stars.

In the deep room where candles burn soundlessly
and peace pours at last through the cells of our bodies,
three of us are watching, one of us is staring
with the wide gaze of a wild sea-fed seal.
Incense and sage speak in smoke loud as waves,
and crickets sing sand towards the edge of the hourglass.
We wait outside time, while time collects courage
around us. The vigil is wordless. Once you

saw time pushing outward, the day in the nursery
when books first meant language, as your mother's voice
traced out the patterns of letters. You saw
words take their breath and the first circles open,
their space collapse inward. They sparkled. Your pen
would scratch ink deliberately, letters incised
like runemarks on stone as you heard, quoting patiently:
Wittgenstein, Gutkind, Gurdjieff, or Weil.

You watch the longest, move the furthest, deliberate in breath,
pulling into your body. You stare towards your death,
head arched on the pillow, your left fingers curled.
Your mouth sucking gently, unmoved by these hours
and their vigil of salt spray, you show us how far
you are going, and how long the long minutes are,
while spiralling night watches over the room
and takes you, until you watch us in turn.

He releases the pages. Here is the mail,
bringing books, gratitude, students, and poems.
Here are kites and the spinning of eternal tops,
icons, parades, monasteries and boardwalks,
gazebos, surprises, loons and unspeaking
silence. Pages again. The words come
like a scent from a flower. Geometry is clear.
Language is natural. The truth is not clever;

cats speak their own language. You are still breathing.
Here is release. Here is your pillow,
cool like a handkerchief pressed in a pocket.
Here is your white tousled long growing hair.
Here is a kiss on your temple to hold you
safe through your solitude's long steady war;

here, you can go. We will stay with you,
loud in the silence we all came here for.

Night, take his left hand, turning the pages.
Spin with the windows and doors that he mended.
Spin with his answers, patient, impatient.
Spin with his dry independence, his arms
warmed by the needs of his family, his hands
flying under the wide, carved gold ring, and the pages
flying so his thought could fly. His breath slows,
lending its edges out to the night.

Here is his open mouth. Silence is here
like a huge brand-new question that he wouldn't answer.
A leaf is his temple. He gazes alone.
He has given his body; his hand lies above
the sheets in a symbol of wholeness, a curve
of thumb and forefinger, ringed with wide gold,
and his face, which is sudden and beautiful, young
for an instant, is new in the light of the flame.

ANDRENA ZAWINSKI

ALTARES

Children empty the mother's house of her,
muscles aching from the weight of her loss
held in their arms so close to their hearts.
Light a candle for them.

Neighbors bemoan an old man lost
to a snowdrift just blocks from his home.
No one ever reported him missing.
Pray on beads for them.

Strangers, heads darting this way and that,
circle a young man on the tracks who slipped
into a heap crossing the street.
Petition the saints for them.

Light candles for them.

Light a candle for girls who gave birth
in the dark the way they conceived,
buried stillborns in deep graves of grief.
Bury your face in your hands for them.

And for the parents whose children fell
to open schoolground fire, who uprooted
wither upon the blood soaked earth.
Lay down wreathes of marigolds for them.

Ring bells for them.

Ring bells for a woman, pack at her heels
with knife, brick, and pipe, who dropped
in the dark, rapt into sleep, then forgot.
Cover the mirrors for them.

Ring bells for the men who balk
at the buck of the rifle butt, drop guns
and run, rogues cast out from the pack.
Raise flags for them. Free doves for them.

And for those with bodies bound by rope,
throats gagged with rags, backs strapped
and lashed, their cries silenced.
Open a window for them.

Deliver oblations for them.

For all the apocalyptic visionaries who leapt
to their ends from bridge rails, or burned drunken
on fumes in the room in a blanket of death.
Let their ashes take wings on the wind for them.

Burn incense for them. Sing chants at altars
you created for them. Carve their names
into stone on monuments you erect to them.
On all the Days of the Dead, remember them.

Remembrance

MARIA SHOCKLEY ERMAN

THE SWEETEST SONG

Perfect little fingers lie flat against my hand
lighter than breath, you occupy my arms.
Silence is your first cry.
Stillness clothes your pale skin, hiding close
in the blanket swaddling you.
I alone face this body
you shed two hours ago
as I thrust you into harsh brilliance
and medical chaos. Then you were a
constant repetition of spikes and valleys on a monitor.
Now you are a line stretching to infinity.
Outside the sun is too much in focus
and despite the absence of bird song,
a sparrow waits on the window sill.
Little girl, I collect your silence,
and rock you into all that I am.
May angels nurse you
into a heaven bereft of me
and celebrate your sweetest cry.

DEBORAH COOPER

FISHING

Was what you loved most,
and when you spoke of it
your eyes, as blue
as any water, filled.

I remember how you talked
about the animals,
the foxes and a doe,
walking right up to you
and looking.

You told me that a wild thing
showing itself
is holy,
in the only way that you could
understand the word.

Today, I fish for you.
It is my first time
and I hear the turtles sing,
plucking the odd strings
of their instruments,
calling for one another.
Above us, eagles
consecrate the sky.

The whole day is made
out of blue
and it is shining

and I remember you telling me this
in your few words
from the bed where you didn't belong.

You, who spent your life
beneath the sky,
lay dying
and dreaming of fishing
and telling us where we might find you
when your body
let you go.

CAROLYN WANGAARD

SEPIA PHOTOGRAPHS

Clouds of black cherry
pipe smoke herald your presence.
I hear your chair squawk
on the front porch.
You sit, book in hand, binding
bare as an unplanted garden,
pages the color of sliced apples
cut yesterday.

"I'm counting cars again," you say.
"Might see someone I know to wave to."
Your green plaid shirt is peppered
with holes from flying pipe ash, the
fabric smooth old flannel.

Your hands are thick, your skin
a cracked mud puddle after
a blazing summer day.
You tell me a story. Your belly shakes
at the punch line, a Model T
turning over.

I recall your velour eyes, wet with tears
and pride seeing the newest one, when you
barely made enough to feed the rest of us.
We talk until fireflies wink in tall grasses,
the humid night draping us in sodden satin.

My memory holds you in white cotton gloves.
Your brown eyes are always laughing.

CHRISTOPHER LOCHE

OFFERINGS

Every Easter we give your brother
flowers, and this year is
no different; a clutch of red
tulips you patiently arrange
by his grave, so the wind
won't knock them over.
I feel muted and strange
at dinner; your parents' kitchen
pastelled in decorations
too cheerful for the absence
they try to cover. Later,
on the interstate, you sleep
beside me, exhausted. But then,
traffic slows. Dream-like, you ask
"What's happening?", and I wish
I didn't know, wish I couldn't see
the ruined body draped in plastic
on the road ahead; I watch
an E.M.T. pick a sneaker off
the highway. I would give anything
for you not to be here, your brother
killed the same way five years ago
in New York, as you and I hiked
through Guatemala— your blame
runs deeper than our love.
"Do you see anything?" you ask,
biting your lip, and I realize
you're looking for him: the contours
of his face, his brown hair pushed

back the way he liked it, his eyes
open with a tenderness that says
there is nothing to forgive.

ANA DOINA

BURIAL RITES

Where I come from
there is an old custom: to bury
the dead under the threshold
to write their names on gates,
or near door hinges;
to keep them close
under step, under eyelids
as if to keep them within reach

their whispers locked in our daily
dust they become
stories of the newborns' lives
whose future they had planned
who dream their dreams.

DEBORAH COOPER

VISITATIONS

On Tuesday
in the produce aisle,
choosing my oranges by feel,
and by their fragrance,
I hear my Granddad
singing in my ear.
An Irish lullaby.
Everything else stops.

There is a tenderness no border can contain.
A web that may be glimpsed
in certain, unexpected plays of light,
or felt
like a shawl
across one's shoulders
laid by unseen hands.

There are sounds in other decibels
the heart can hear
when the wind is right
and the mind has quieted its clicking.
The border guards are sleeping
at their stations.
Spirits come and go.

The wall between the living and the dead
is as yielding as a membrane,
is as porous as a skin.
Lay your palm against it

and you can hear their voices
in your hand
and in the place where the chest opens
like a flower.

They are not far away,
no farther than the breath
and enter us as easily,
in pine and peonies,
in oranges and rain.
Our mouths fall open in surprise,
a quiet radiance
erupting
in our eyes.

D.J. LACHANCE

THE FALL

Two souls fell from above. Disgorged from a dead machine, they joined the wreckage on its journey down.

One, screamed and thrashed at the air, only becoming peaceful after grasping a part of the craft that had only so recently been aloft. Together, they continued their plunge.

The other, followed the new path and felt a sunlit cloud, briefly led a flock of geese and danced with autumn's leaves.

At journey's end, both died.

BIOGRAPHIES

CHARLOTTE G. ARNOLD lives in Northumberland, England. Her work has appeared in several publications and she is currently working on a novel. *Saturday* was written after what seemed to be a year of endless deaths and losses.

BARRY BALLARD received his M.A. from Texas Christian University in 1983. He has a strong preference for writing contemporary sonnets and has enjoyed publication in a number of literary journals. His first collection entitled *Green Tombs to Jupiter* won the Snail's Pace Press poetry award for 1999.

MARK BLICKLEY is a playwright with eleven New York production credits. He has published stories, plays, and essays in books, magazines and journals across the country. A collection of his short fiction, *The World's Greatest Saxophone Player,* is forthcoming from the Red Hen Press. His newest play, *Beauty Knows No Pain,* which opened in New York last June, was selected for this year's Edinburgh Fringe Festival in Scotland.

BILL BROWN teaches literature and creative writing in Nashville. His poetry has been published in many journals including, *The Literary Review, Passages North, Zone Three,* and *The English Journal.* He has published three collections of poems, *Holding on by Letting Go, What the Night Told Me,* and, most recently, *The Art of Dying.* He co-authored (along with Malcolm Glass) a writing textbook, *Important Words, for Poets and Writers.*

DEBORAH COOPER has been published in many literary journals and anthologies including *North Coast Review, Rag Mag, ArtWord Quarterly* and *The Wolf Head Quarterly.* She uses poetry extensively in her work as a Chaplain in St. Mary's Hospice Program and regularly conducts workshops on the interfacing of poetry and spirituality. Currently, she is guest editor for the North Coast Review.

Liz Crow is a writer and broadcaster based in the United Kingdom. Her work has been published and broadcast by *The Disability Press, Rough Guides, The Women's Press* and BBC radio and television, among others.

Ruth Daigon was a professional singer for many years, first in Canada, then in New York as a Columbia Recording Artist, a guest artist on CBS's *Camera Three* and a soloist with the New York Pro Musica. In the late seventies, she made the transition from concert soprano to full time poet, editor and performance artist. Her most recent book, *Between One Future And The Next,* Papier-Mache Press, was published in 1995. Her latest book, *The Moon Inside,* was published by Graviry/Newton's Baby in December 1999.

Ana Doina was born in Romania when the country was under communist regime. She graduated with an M.A. in Philosophy and History from the University of Bucharest. Recently, her poems have been published and/or are forthcoming in journals and anthologies, including *Timber Creek Review, Icarus, Chiron Review, Clockpunchers: Poetry of America's Workplace* and *American Diaspora: Poetry of Exile.*

Mary H. Eastham is a poet, short story writer and performance artist. Her work has been published in many publications, including *Paris Transcontinental, Pearl, Mediphors, Nerve Cowboy,* and *Family Celebrations.* She was recently a featured poet at the Austin International Poetry Festival 2000 and a winner of the 2000 Allen Ginsberg Poetry Awards.

MARIA SHOCKLEY ERMAN has been published in *Westview, Kimera,* and *Green Hills Literary Lantern.*

KAREN ETHELSDATTAR is a poet and liturgist. Her poetry has been published in many publications, including *Woman Spirit, Off Our Backs, Dark Horse, Calyx,* and the Papier-Mache Press anthologies, *If I Had My Life to Live Over I Would Pick More Daisies* and *At Our Core: Women Writing about Power.*

ANNIE FINCH is the author of *Eve* and the narrative poem, *Marie Moving,* both from Story Line Press, and *The Ghost of Meter,* University of Michigan Press. She has edited several anthologies, including *A Formal Feeling Comes: Poems in Form by Contemporary Women,* now in its third printing, and *An Exaltation of Forms: Contemporary Poets Celebrate the Diversity of Their Art.* Her website is www.muohio.edu/~finchar.

CAROLYN BRIGIT FLYNN was educated at George Washington University and the University of California, Los Angeles. Her work has appeared in many publications, including *Calyx: A Journal of Art and Literature by Women, Black Buzzard Review, Earth's Daughters,* the anthologies *New to North America: Writing by U.S. Immigrants, Intimate Kisses: The Poetry of Sexual Pleasure* and Deena Mertzger's *Writing for Your Life.* She teaches writing workshops called "Writing to Feed the Soul."

JOHN GREY is an Australian born poet, playwright and musician. He has been published recently in *Whetstone, Bottomfish* and *South Carolina Review* and has work upcoming in *Weber Studies* and *New Collage.*

ROBERT WATERS GREY, a native of Maryland, is a graduate of Brown University and The University of Virginia. His collection of poetry, *Saving The Dead*, was published by Briarpatch Press. His poetry and stories have been published in many journals, including *Pittsburgh Quarterly, Kansas Quarterly, Hollins Critic, Willow Review* and *The Iconoclast*. Currently, he is on the faculty of the creative writing program at UNC Charlotte.

HOLLY HAGEN recently graduated from Kent State University's program in English with a minor in creative writing. She will be attending Southampton College in New York to pursue her M.F.A. in creative writing. Holly is also a survivor of a serious car crash that took the life of her boyfriend, Brendan R. Daugherty.

RICHARD HAIN lost a baby sister when he was three (cot death). At sixteen, he found the baby son of a church leader dead in his pram, presumably another cot death. He became a Christian partly as a response to this experience, went on to become a doctor and now works as a pediatric palliative care physician in the United Kingdom.

ALBERT HALEY is the author of *Home Ground: Stories of Two Families and the Land* and the novel, *Exotic*. His short fiction has appeared in many publications including, *The New Yorker, The Atlantic Monthly,* and *Image*. He has served as writer in residence at Abilene Christian University since 1997. Last year he collaborated with a classical pianist to produce "The Thanatos Negotiations," a concert of music and poetry that speaks to the emotional and philosophical complications of death.

ZYSKANDAR A. JAIMOT has been widely published in Europe and the Americas. Of poetry, he says, "Poetry to me is like the night, where dreams become sweaty sticky sonnets which you peel off your skin at dawn."

D.J. LACHANCE has been published in U.S. and Japanese literary and special interest magazines, including *Art Forum, Poettalk, BookLovers, The Plaza and Pleiades.* Though multifaceted, "The Fall" stems from having lived with reasonable expectations of not surviving the Gulf War; his Army unit was collectively and individually hunted by a terrorist group during the war.

CHRISTOPHER LOCHE received his M.F.A. from Goddard College. He recently received a poetry scholarship from Foundacion Valparaiso in Spain. His poems have been published in many journals, including *The Sun, The Literary Review, Connecticut Review* and *Hubbub.* His chapbook, *How To Burn,* is available from Adastra Press.

GIOVANNI MALITO is a Canadian who has been working in Ireland as a Lecturer in Chemistry for the past five years. He edits *The Brobdingnagian Times* and co-edits *Tableau.* Recent publication credits include *Curious Rooms, Sulphur River Literary Review* and *The Iconoclast.*

CAROL MALLEY has been published in many journals and anthologies, including a poem and short story in *When a Lifemate Dies: Stories of Love, Loss, & Healing,* Fairview Press. She is a journalist for a daily newspaper and poetry editor of *Peregrine* literary journal. She leads writing workshops for children and adults.

JAMES A. MCGRATH is an artist, poet and teacher. He created the narrative poetry for the PBS American Indian Artist Series: *Loloma, Houser, Scholder, Gorman, Hardin, Lonewolf* and *Medicine Flower.* He has been published in *MAN! Magazine, Dakota Territory, Art in the Navaho Universe* and *Arizona Highways.*

Ann E. Michael is a PA Council on the Arts 1998 Poetry Fellowship recipient, poet, librettist, and an essayist whose work has appeared in print, on-line and on the radio. Recently her work has appeared in *Minimus, Sidewalks Magazine, Buckle & Icarus 2000* and in several anthologies.

Marllee Millman has her Ph.B. in Communications from Northwestern University. Having had to journey through widowhood without resources that spoke from a widow's point of view, she wrote her own.

Noel Nowosielski was born in Leeds, England where he still lives with his partner, Pippa. He lost his mother at the age of twelve. This loss has informed not only his writing, but also his work as a social worker. His first collection of poetry, *Czech Out The Ladies,* was published in 1996. A second collection, *Where Did I Leave My Heart?,* was published in May 2000.

Estelle Padawer is a member of Bergen Poets and Main Street Poets. Her poems have been published in many anthologies and small presses.

Marianne Poloskey has been published in many journals, including *War, Literature & the Arts, Writer to Writer* and *Christian Science Monitor.* Forthcoming publications include *Medicinal Purposes Literary Review, Hidden Oak Poetry Journal,* and the anthologies, *American Diaspora: Poetry of Exile,* Univ. of Iowa Press, and *Clockpunchers: Poetry of the American Workplace,* Partisan Press.

Jane Rohrer is the Vice-President of Academic Affairs at Sierra Nevada College, Incline Village, NV. She has always been fascinated with the human condition. As she has observed and participated in the process of her parents' aging, she has taken comfort in being able to write poetry to record the process. Her father died at the age of 79 and her mother is 96, living in a retirement village.

SHANNON SEXTON is a senior sociology major at Hiram College in Hiram, Ohio. She plans on attending graduate school to pursue a Master of Fine Arts in Poetry and Creative Fiction.

SUSAN TAYLOR is an M.F.A. candidate in the Creative Writing program at the University of Minnesota, Twin Cities, thanks, in part, to an Edelstein-Keller fellowship. Her work has appeared in *Rosebud, Binx Street, CWC Journal* and *Cal State Los Angeles Statement* and will be included in an anthology of short-short fiction to be published by Sprout Press.

PAMELA USCHUK is the author of *Finding Peaches in the Desert*, a book of poetry which has just been released by Wings Press. This fall, a CD with her poetry and music by Joy Harjo is also due to be released. Her poetry has been published in many journals and anthologies, including *Poetry, Commonweal, The American Voice, 48 Younger American Poets* and *One Earth*. She teaches poetry workshops and literature at the University of Arizona's Writing Works Center.

LINDA VAUGHAN is a psychotherapist and poet residing in Colorado. She has had numerous poems published in *Buffalo Bones*, a national poetry quarterly.

CAROLYN WANGAARD is the founding editor of the quarterly poetry journal, *Buffalo Bones* and co-editor in chief of the Evergreen Women's Press. She is the editor of two anthologies and has received national recognition for her writing.

Rogan Wolf is a free-lance social worker, who works and lives in London. He founded the charity called "Action for the Education and Advancement of Social Responsibility," soon to be called "Social Groundwork." Its website can be found at www.charts.force9.co.uk

Andrena Zawinski is the author of *Traveling in Reflected Light*. Her poetry has been published in many journals, including *Kalliope, Nimrod International, Gulf Coast* and *Quarterly West*. She is currently working, free-lance, in the San Francisco Bay Area and is Features Editor at www.poetrymagazine.com. Her poem, *Altares*, previously appeared in HEArt.

Death, Loss and Bereavement Resources

American Hospice Foundation –
The American Hospice Foundation offers on-site training workshops for managers, employee assistant professionals, educators, bereavement counselors, and mental health professionals. They also have many helpful publications on grief.
Contact:
United States - (202) 223-0204   Website: www.americanhospice.org

National Hospice and Palliative Care Organization –
The National Hospice and Palliative Care Organization is the largest nonprofit membership organization representing hospice and palliative care programs and professionals in the United States. The organization is committed to improving end of life care and expanding access to hospice care with the goal of profoundly enhancing quality of life for people dying and their loved ones.
Contact:
United States toll-free - (800) 658-8898 Website: www.nhpco.org
United Kingdom - (+44)(0) 20-7520-8299 Website: www.hospice-spc-council.org.uk

The Compassionate Friends –
The Compassionate Friends is a national nonprofit, self-help support organization that offers friendship and understanding to families who are grieving the death of a child of any age, from any cause. There is no religious affiliation. There are no membership fees or dues and all bereaved family members are welcome.
Contact:
United States - (630) 990-0010 Website: www.compassionatefriends.org
United Kingdom - 011-44-117-953-9639
Canada - (204) 475-9527

Colophon

This book was printed in an edition of 5,000 copies

Designed by Don Eddy

Type is Adobe Garamond and Adobe Garamond Expert
Composed on a Macintosh 9500 using Adobe Pagemaker 6.01

Printed on
Westminster Natural - 360 ppi
Antique finish - by Georgia Pacific

by

Patterson Printing Company